Options Trading

Tips & Tricks for Your Profit Maximization

JOE BRONSKI

Copyright © 2016 Franky | studio
All rights reserved.
ISBN: 1537200658
ISBN-13: 978-1537200651

© **Copyright 2016 by Franky | studio - All rights reserved.**

This document is presented with the desire to provide reliable, quality information about the topic in question and the facts discussed within. This eBook is sold under the assumption that neither the author nor the publisher should be asked to provide the services discussed within. If any discussion, professional or legal, is otherwise required a proper professional should be consulted.

This Declaration was held acceptable and equally approved by the Committee of Publishers and Associations as well as the American Bar Association.

The reproduction, duplication or transmission of any of the included information is considered illegal whether done in print or electronically. Creating a recorded copy or a secondary copy of this work is also prohibited unless the action of doing so is first cleared through the Publisher and condoned in writing. All rights reserved.

Any information contained in the following pages is considered accurate and truthful and that any liability through inattention or by any use or misuse of the topics discussed within falls solely on the reader. There are no cases in which the Publisher of this work can be held responsible or be asked to provide reparations for any loss of monetary gain or other damages which may be caused by following the presented information in any way shape or form.

The following information is presented purely for informative purposes and is therefore considered universal. The information presented within is done so without a contract or any other type of assurance as to its quality or validity.

Any trademarks which are used are done so without consent and any use of the same does not imply consent or permission was gained from the owner. Any trademarks or brands found within are purely used for clarification purposes and no owners are in anyway affiliated with this work.

Table of Contents

Introduction 6
Chapter 1: Mistakes to Avoid When Trading Riskier Options 8
Chapter 2: Reasons You Need an Order Flow Tracking Program 12
Chapter 3: Double Diagonal Strategy 16
Chapter 4: Leveraged Covered Call Strategy 20
Chapter 5: Skip Strike Butterfly Spread Strategy 24
Chapter 6: Front Spread Strategy 28
Conclusion 32

Fast Memorization Techniques: 36
Introduction 38
Chapter 1: Why Memorization is Difficult and How to Help Yourself 40
Chapter 2: Preparing Your Body 44
Chapter 3: A Few Other Techniques 46
Conclusion 49

Introduction

Congratulations on downloading *Option Trading: Advanced Tips & Tricks for Your Profit Maximization* and thank you for doing so. Understanding enough about options trading to feel comfortable moving from intermediate to advanced options trading strategies is a big step and one you should be congratulated for making. This will only get more complicated from here, however, and it is important to understand that you still have a long way to go in terms of both practice and strategy comprehension before you are ready to trade at the highest levels.

You are well on your way, however, and much farther along than most people will ever get; which is why the following chapters will discuss everything you need to know to trade riskier options with higher potentials for reward successfully as well as the right tools to ensure you are on the right side of virtually every trade. You will then learn the specific details of the double diagonal strategy, the leveraged covered call strategy, the skip strike butterfly spread strategy and the front spread strategy. Stick with your dedication to options trading and you will go far, your hard work is getting closer to paying off every day.

There are plenty of books on this subject on the market, thanks again for choosing this one! Every effort was made to ensure it is full of as much useful information as possible, please enjoy!

Here you will find the tools used by me!

- **_Binary Options Trading Signals Live!_**

Binary Options Trading Signals Is The Premier Signal Service For Binary Options As You Watch A Live Trader With Over 10 Years Of Experience! Promote This And Your Users Will Absolutely Love You

- *Binary Options Pro Signals*

Binary Options Pro Signals Is The Best Way To Trade Markets! Customers Love The Product Because Of Its Ease Of Use. Profits Can Be Made In As Little As One Hour.

- *Real Money Doubling Forex Robot Fap Turbo*

Fapturbo Is The Only Automated Forex Income Solution That Doubles Real Monetary Deposits In Under 30 Days.

- *Quantum Binary Signals Subscription*

Quantum Binary Signals Is The Leading Signals Provider For Binary Options Forex, Stocks And Commodities.

Chapter 1: Mistakes to Avoid When Trading Riskier Options

Inexperienced traders are often warned away from purchasing options that are out of the money as being a greater risk than the ultimate reward is likely to be. While it is true that a short expiration time coupled with an out of the of money option will frequently look appealing, especially to those with a smaller amount of trading capital to work with, the issue is that all of these types of options are likely to look equally appealing which leaves them with no way to tell the good from the bad. As a more experienced trader, however, you have many more tools at your disposal than the average novice which means that, while risky, cheap options have the potential to generate substantial returns, as long as you keep the following in mind while trading them.

Ignoring the difference between historical volatility and implied volatility: Implied volatility should be one of the main gauges you use to determine if a given option is priced appropriately. As a rule, the higher the amount of implied volatility, the more bearish the market is going to be and the more expensive various options will be. However, it should not be the only thing that you take into account which means that historical volatility is just as crucial when it comes to choosing profitable cheap options correctly. You can study the

historical volatility of a given option by plotting it out beforehand in order to determine the difference between the general volatility and the current amount of volatility.

Ignoring the probability: Always remember that the historical data will not apply to the current trends in the market at all times which means you will always want to consider the probability as well as the odds that the market is going to behave the way it typically does. The odds are how likely the market is to behave as expected and the probability is the ratio of the likelihood of a given outcome. Understanding the probability of certain outcomes can make it easy to purchase the proper options to minimize losses related to holdings of specific underlying stocks. When purchasing cheap options, it is important to remember that they are always going to be cheap for a reason as price is determined by strike price of the underlying stock as well as the amount of time remaining for the option to regain its value, choose wisely otherwise you are doing little more than gambling and there are certainly better ways to gamble than via options trading.

Ignoring the importance of the delta: Everyone knows that if the delta of the option you are considering is near 1, then you will want to generate calls and if it is near -1 then you will want to generate puts. When it comes to cheap options, however, you will want to choose options with a higher delta as they are more likely to conform with the expectations you might have in relation to the underlying stock which means you will see greater gains when the underlying stock does, in fact, begin to move.

Choosing the wrong parameters: When it comes to choosing options related to front month contracts, it is important to keep in mind the timeframe for any expectations you have on the underlying stock. While certain options will always be alluring, it is important to not get suckered into an unreasonable timeframe that will not reasonably pay off in the way that you would ultimately hope it would. Additionally, regardless of what timeframe you choose, it is important to maintain a realistic set of expectations when it comes to the movement of the underlying stock as, depending on the timeframe, it can be possible for the stock to see a fair amount of fluctuation before any related options expire.

Not using sentiment analysis: Sentiment analysis is often overlooked by many traders which is unfortunate as using it properly is a good way to determine how likely it is that the current trend of the underlying stock will continue until the end of the given option. This means it is important to always observe instances of short interest as well as put activity and analyst ratings to get a fair idea of underlying stock price movement in the near term. When using sentiment analysis, it can be easy to get lost in the gut reactions that the market can have to major events. This is why it is always a more profitable choice to wait for the initial wave of panic to pass before jumping in close enough to the ground floor to make a profit.

Ignoring technical indicators: When it comes to choosing cheap options, it is important to avoid making any snap judgements, even if you are generally fairly apt at spotting a good value in  more traditional option trading scenarios. Always remember that mind that anything that can be said to be easy money will in most situations already have been picked up by one of the major players which means that the profit to be found in what's left is going to take in-depth analysis of related stocks as well as relevant technical indicators as possible.

Don't forget to determine the extrinsic value as compared to the intrinsic value: The extrinsic value can be thought of as the difference between the current price an option is going for on the market and its intrinsic, or inherent value based on the guaranteed premiums that it is going to return, even if it expires or if the underlying stock does not move at all. While the intrinsic value is always considered, when it comes to deciding which cheaper options are worth considering, the extrinsic value becomes increasingly important because it decreases in value the closer the option is to expiring.

Keep commission costs in mind: If you are planning to develop a strategy around cheap options, then it is important to ensure that your broker has a reasonable process in place for doing so. When you begin to contemplate a strategy based on cheap options then what you are really doing is setting up a strategy based around the idea of high risk and high rewards which means you are likely going to need to place quite a few more trades then you might otherwise have done before. Commissions on trades add up quickly, don't let yourself be burned.

Treating stop losses carelessly: While it is an easy choice to place a stop loss on an option that has quite a bit of capital riding on it. A mistake that many advanced traders make is to somehow still manage to underestimate its importance of placing them carefully on cheap options just because there is less perceived as being available to lose. While this is true on an individual basis, remember, the quantity of the trades you make is likely to go up if you are pursing cheap options, while the quality of each trade is likely to go down as well. As such, without taking preventative measures you can find yourself burning capital faster than you otherwise might expect.

Trying to adapt a strategy: Even if you have previously had a fair amount of success when it comes to high risk and high reward options, it is important that, rather than adapting an existing strategy, you instead create an entirely new strategy built around taking the most advantage of the unique benefits of cheap options while at the same time minimizing their unique risks. While you might be tempted to put your skills to the test and start trading, taking the time to create a new strategy will always produce more profitable results in the long run.

Chapter 2: Reasons You Need an Order Flow Tracking Program

Order Flow Sequencing was created by a master trader who worked at many of the major firms including the likes of such giants in the field as Sungard Capital Markets and Bear Sterns. Order flow sequencing is used to document and track prices that the major players in  any market are going to make moves at. This information, in turn, provides advanced traders the ability to determine potential liquidity as well as any risks that might be associated with it with a greater level of accuracy when it comes to determining the mood of the market as a whole.

To understand the benefits of order flow processing, it can help to think of the major players in your market of choice as the casino that you, as an individual trader, are playing in. This means they are the house and the house always wins which means that if you trade against them, you might win in the short term, but you will always loose out in the end. As such, it is often better to trade in

their wake and collect the smaller, more reliable profits, then betting against them in the hopes of winning big.

Major players are typically quite easy to spot, they are banks, both merchant and traditional, as well as hedge funds, investment firms, financial institutions, commercial traders and even world governments. If there is a player in the market you prefer whose actions can unilaterally change the direction of the market, then you always want to know what that player is going to do next. Additionally, understanding the trends that these players create can make it much easier for you determine the best time for you to make a move and when the best time to place your own trades is likely going to be.

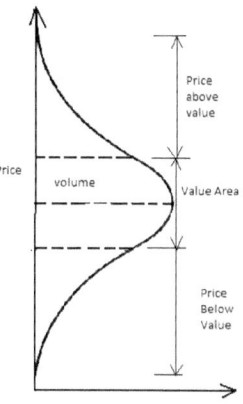

Order flow sequencing first gained mass acceptance in the early 1900s when understanding the importance of information generated by the market first began to gain popularity. The reason it is just as effective today is that even when compared with more modern indicator methods it presents you with information earlier on in the market cycle when you can more easily capitalize on emerging trends to your own advantage. Nevertheless, relatively few traders take the time to utilize this extremely versatile and effective method, simply because it requires its own tools. Ensure you aren't among them by keeping the following in mind.

Value area

In order to understand order flow sequencing, you must first understand value areas. A value area is the easiest way to determine how the major players in your chosen market are going to move and to what degree. Value area can be broken down into a few core parts, the Control point, the High point and the Low point. Levels in the high value area are those where the volume as well as the demand of trades has drastically increased the price substantially. Low value areas are points where the volume and the demand for trades has decreased to the point the underlying asset is again consider a good deal. The control point is the price as you are looking at it in the moment.

These values can either be tracked with a volume profile tool that is provided by the trading platform that you favor, or you can choose one of the many available online, that works with the platform of your choice. Regardless, once you do begin looking at various values of volume it is important to look for points that overlap between the control point and the high value areas. This should also line up with previous low value areas for the best results. Areas of overlap are areas of potential interest which gives you a good idea of where you want to spend your pre-open market hours finding out more about so you don't have to do it on the fly as the market is actually moving.

You will likely want to consider the estimated value early on in your analysis phase as it can be done relatively quickly and easily and can give you a clear idea of where the market may move next. Low volume is a good indicator that a shift is coming soon and rejection at one price point, increases the likelihood of rejection at another. Keeping an eye on volume will also give you an additional amount of confirmation once the major players in the market do actually begin buying. These guidelines are likely to remain accurate throughout the front month if not longer.

Tracking sequences in the order flow
Once you have a clear idea of various value variables, you will then want to begin tracking orders as they appear to watch the volume as it continues to grow which will make it clear how various entry and exit points are likely to remain profitable. This is the same information that you would receive by using a candlestick report, except that this way you can watch it form instead of responding to it after the fact. Establishing the right value areas means you can easily monitor various instances of order flow to determine the points of maximum profit.

When using this process, you want to set aside time every morning before the markets open to ensure that specific value zones, and their volumes, are where you expect them to be. With

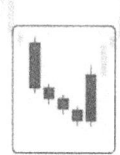

this done, you are going to want to then determine the points where the various low value and high value areas align to targeted levels and then act accordingly.

When it comes to seeing if tracking order flow sequences works for you, a great place to start if your platform does not offer these features is with Jigsaw Tools available at JigsawTrading.com for free. These tools can track the stock, forex and futures market and offer up plenty of functionality including DOM and Time sales.

Chapter 3: Double Diagonal Strategy

To take advantage of the double diagonal strategy, you are going to want to start by running a diagonal put spread at the same time you are running a diagonal call spread. Remember, in a diagonal spread, you want to take a horizontal spread based on time and move the long leg to an alternate strike point. It is called a diagonal spread because the legs do not have the same month.

In a diagonal call spread, you will want to cross a sort call spread with a long calendar spread which means you are going to want to make a move based on time decay. After you have sold off the second call at the first strike point you will have legged yourself into a spread for the short call. This will help you to generate a net credit which means that once you sell the second call you will be making a pure profit. The same theory goes for a diagonal put, though obviously the specifics are going to be quite different.

Running the double diagonal
With this in mind, you are going to want to start by using both the diagonal put spread as well as the diagonal all spread which allows you to take advantage of the accelerated time decay that inherently comes with front-month options when compared to the more measured pace you can find with back-month options. You perform this strategy by doing the following:

1. You start by purchasing a put that is out of the money at a given strike price that is 2 months from expiring.

2. At the same time, you are going to want to sell a put that is out of the money at another profitable strike price that is 30 days from expiring.

3. You will also want to sell a call that is out of the money at

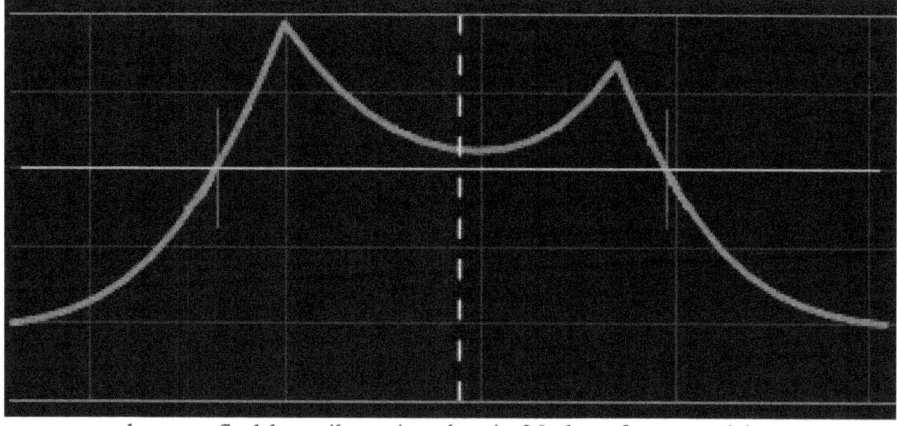

another profitable strike price that is 30 days from expiring.

4. You will also want to purchase a call at another profitable strike price that is not going to expire for 60 days.

Ideally, the underlying stock price is going to remain between the boundaries of 2 and 3. If the price is still above those strike prices then you are going to want to sell the options that are 30 days from expiring while also selling another put at the first beneficial strike price and selling another call at the second beneficial strike price that expires the same time as 4 above. Always remember that when graphing this strategy, your loss and profit lines are not going to be straight because the options that are 60 days from expiring are still open. Hard angles or straight lines are possible when all of the options used in a given strategy expire at the same time.

While this strategy might seem extremely complicated at first, it can be made to seem much more manageable if you instead consider it as a form of profiting from a neutral amount of movement in the market, simply spread out into multiple expiration cycles.

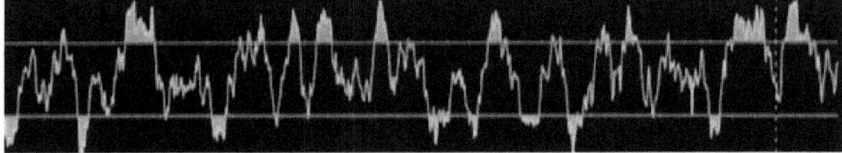

Successful execution
The best time to establish this strategy is when the underlying stock has moved half way between the strike price of 2 and 3, and ideally as close to the midpoint between the two as possible. This is because if the stock is not at this center point then the strategy is likely to have either a bearish or a bullish bias because of it. You will want the stock to remain at this point so the options you sold will expire worthlessly while you still capture as much premium as possible.

This means that the first put you purchased as well as the last call you purchased will work to reduce your overall risk in case the underlying stock moves more than you expected in either direction. Likewise, the goal of this strategy should be to generate a net credit, though this can be easier said than done. This is because the options that are set to expire in the front month have less available time value than the options that are two months out. This means the better option might actually be to decide to go for a net debit instead and then to make up the difference in costs by 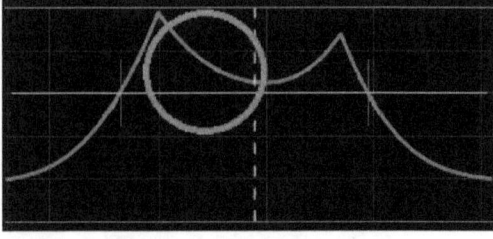 selling the second pair of options after the first have expired.

When the front month options reach a point where their expiration is imminent, you will want the underlying stock price to be somewhere between 2 and 3. When this is the case it is important to always buy to close the first pair of options and also to sell an additional put at the second strike price and another call at the third strike price. This round of options should all expire at the same time as 1 and 4 above. This strategy is referred to as rolling out.

Finishing up
It is common for many traders to purchase options that are near the front month as they don't wish to deal with the extra risk that comes with a Friday night expiration. This makes it easier to prevent additional price swings between the point the market closes and the point it opens again. Additionally, after you have sold of the extra options you purchased relating to strike prices 2 and 3, you will essentially be in a basic iron condor scenario.

This means you are going to want the underlying stock price to stay where it has been as it will allow the remaining options to expire after they are out of the money which means you can simply pocket the various premiums that are coming to you from various points in the double diagonal. This is what makes the double diagonal preferable to a longer iron condor in many traders' eyes, in this scenario you also get to take the premium relate to the short options at the second and third strike price, not just once, but twice.

Chapter 4: Leveraged Covered Call Strategy

The leveraged covered call is also known as the fig leaf strategy or the LEAPS diagonal spread. As this name implies, it helps to cover some of the risk that can occur through the use of Long Term Equity Anticipation Securities (LEAPS). The average LEAPS call will expire in more than a year's time which means a call in the short term would be somewhere around 45 days. Additionally, this is a good strategy to employ when you feel mildly bullish about the market as it stands and when looking towards the future.

Running the fig leaf strategy
When you purchase a LEAPS call, you are gaining access to the ability to purchase the underlying stock at the first strike price you are going to want to keep in mind. You then want to sell a call at a favorable strike price so that you can sell the underlying stock for a profit if you find yourself assigned.

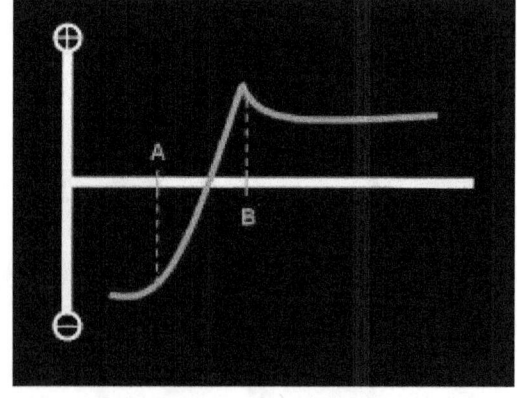

The goal in this strategy is to provide a covered call for a LEAPS transaction which is, in and of itself, a stand in for actually owning the stock in question. While the two actions are largely similar, the fact that there are two separate expiration dates in this instance makes it more complicated, but also potentially much more profitable when compared to the standard covered call. It is important to understand that when

1. Start by purchasing a LEAPS call at a price that is in the money, the first strike price discussed above.

2. You will then want to sell an out of the money call in the short term at the second strike price outlined above. You will want the underlying stock price to remain closer to the second strike price as opposed to the first.

It is important to keep in mind that when graphing this strategy, your loss and profit lines are not going to be straight because the LEAPS call will still remain open until after the shorter call will expire. Hard angles or straight lines are possible when all of the options used in a given strategy expire at the same time. Additionally, it is important to always remember that calculating potential profits when you begin utilizing this strategy is difficult because this data will not reliably be available until you have a clear idea of how the LEAPS call is going to perform as well as what premium is going to be generated after any short calls are sold.

Fig leaf goals

Your goals while using the fig leaf strategy should be to buy a LEAPS call that will likely move in similar ways to the underlying stock. This means you are going to want to consider calls that automatically have a delta of .8, if not higher. To find options with this level of delta you are generally going to need to consider options that are 20 percent in the money if not more. If you are looking for an underlying stock with high volatility, you will likely need an option that is 40 percent in the money instead.

This strategy is favored by some options traders over the more traditional covered call as this way you aren't required to put up all of the required capital up front as you would if you purchased the underlying stock up front. As such, and premium that you make when selling the call, you created, will be a larger overall percentage of your initial investment which means your profits will be proportionally higher as leverage is applied to the potential return.

Fig leaf strategy risks

While this strategy has additional benefits when compared to a standard covered call, there are also additional risks to consider as well. The biggest of these is that unlike when you are purchasing underlying stock, LEAPS will expire, this won't be soon, of course, but when they finally do, your entire investment could go with it if you aren't careful.

Additionally, while getting assigned on a short option is irrelevant at worst with a covered call, or even beneficial in some cases, when using the fig leaf strategy, being assigned on a short call can be cumbersome because you are not actually in possession of the stock in question yet. Remember, having the right to purchase something, and actually purchasing it can be a world apart if you are not prepared while options trading.

This is because exercising the option to buy on the long LEAPS call would be a poor choice because of all of the related time value that you would instantly lose by doing so. Unfortunately, this then leaves you best option to be to simply hope the short call you made will be out of the money at its expiration date so you can sell it multiple times before the LEAPS based call finally expires to make up the difference.

Fig leaf tips
It can be effective to use this strategy if you have a clear idea of how a certain expensive underlying stock is likely to move but can't afford a traditional option.

If the underlying stock price jumps the strike price of the shorter option ahead of its expiration date, then closing out the entire option might be a reliable choice as if you have done everything correctly this should result in a profit being made on the trade.

When you are assigned on the short call you are going to want to avoid exercising on the LEAPS call and instead sell it on the open market as a way of profiting from all of the inherent time value. At the same time, you would then want to purchase the related stock to ensure you can adequately cover a short position related to said stock.

The best place for the underlying stock to be in this strategy is as close to the strike price that the short option has as possible while also not increasing past it excessively.

Chapter 5: Skip Strike Butterfly Spread Strategy

Skip strike butterfly call spread
A skip strike butterfly call spread is a strategy that is more directionally focused than a more traditional butterfly spread. With a skip strike butterfly call spread you are going to be looking for underlying stock prices that increase, though not beyond the point of your second strike price. In this instance the calls related to the second and fourth strike points will be practically zero though you will still retain the premium generated from the call at the original strike price.

This strategy works by placing a spread for a short call into a butterfly long call spread which means you are more or less unloading the spread of the short call in order to finance the butterfly. This in turn would require selling and also buying a call with the same strike price, you can simply skip this step as the outcome is always going to be moot.

Furthermore, the spread for the short call makes it possible to set up this strategy for little additional cost and at a significant gain. There is also going to be additional risk because of it, which makes the whole affair riskier than a common butterfly spread. To perform a skip strike butterfly call spread, you will want to do the following while keeping in mind that all of the strike prices should be the same distance from one another and also expire in the same month. Additionally, you will want the underlying stock price to remain near or lower than the initial strike point.

Using the skip strike butterfly call spread

1. Establish an initial profitable strike price and purchase a call there.

2. Sell two additional calls at a second strike price

3. You will then want to ignore the third strike price

4. Purchase a call at the fourth strike price

Additional considerations
This is a great strategy to use if you are interested in minimizing risk, then using this strategy with the assuming that the price will stay around the first strike price means that the underlying stock would need to move significantly before you begin to see any major losses. This risk can further be mitigated by using it with index options as opposed to traditional options because indexes are even less volatile than individual underlying stocks with low volatility because various price movements tend to cancel out major movement in either direction.

This is a good strategy to consider if you are bullish on the current state of the market and what it is going to look like in the near future. You will be able to break even at the point the options expire if you are looking for a net profit assuming you hit the third strike price as it should generate a net credit. The most profitable the trade can be is if you exercise at the precise moment the

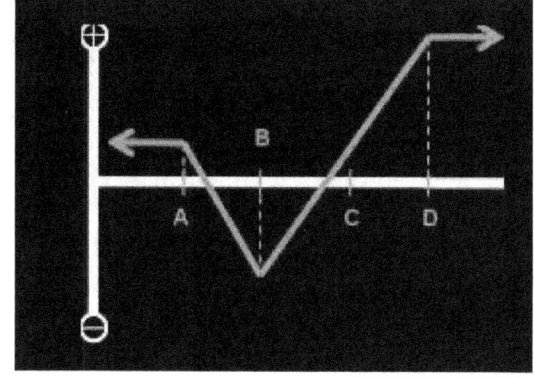

stock reaches the second of your strike prices. The most you can make on this strategy is the second strike price subtracted by the first strike price will credits and debits taken into account.

Skip strike butterfly put spread

Like the skip strike butterfly call spread, the skip strike butterfly put spread is a more strongly directional strategy than a more traditional butterfly spread. The biggest difference is that instead of looking for an underlying stock increase, you are hoping for the underlying stock price to instead decrease a specific amount, but not beyond the third strike price that you set. This makes it a good strategy to use if you are bearish, but only slightly bearish as you don't want the price of the underlying stock to decrease past the point that you will make a profit on it. If all goes according to plan, then you will not make any money off of puts that are near the first and second strike prices but you will make a premium for the put at the fourth strike point.

This strategy works by placing a short put spread into a longer put butterfly spread which means you are selling the shorter of the put spreads to pay for the longer one. As with the skip strike butterfly call spread, you can avoid the requisite buying and selling at the second strike point as it will ultimately cancel itself out. Additionally, the short spread will make it possible to use this particular strategy to generate a positive credit or a small amount of debit. Unfortunately, it also adds an additional layer of risk to the proceedings than you would see when using the more standard traditional butterfly.

Use the skip strike butterfly put spread

1. You want to start by purchasing a put at the first strike price you are interested in. Always remember that all of the strike prices must be equidistant from one another and all expire in the same month.

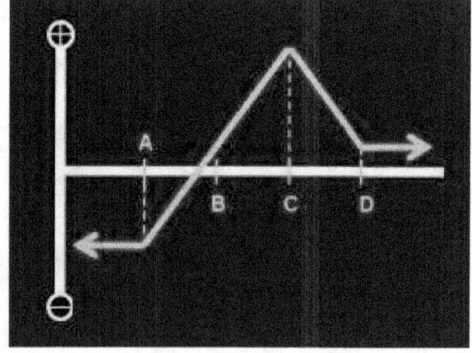

2. You can skip the second price as the resulting buy and selling always cancel one another out.

3. You will then want to sell two puts at the third strike price.

4. Next you will need to buy a put that is at the fourth strike price. Throughout this process you are going to want to ensure that the underlying stock price is always at the fourth strike point or higher for the best results.

Additional considerations

The point of maximum profit for this strategy is the moment the underlying stock price hits the third strike price. The total amount of profit possible is ultimately limited to the difference of the fourth strike price and the third strike price after any additional debits or credits have been factored in. If you hope to break even at the point the option expires while still generating a credit, then you will need an underlying stock price of the second strike price. Likewise, if the trade was established for a net debit, then you can break even either at the fourth strike point or the second strike point once debits have been taken into account.

Chapter 6: Front Spread Strategy

Call front spread

The call front spread strategy allows you to purchase a call that is at the money or slightly below the money at a discounted price compared to purchasing the option on its own. Furthermore, the ultimate goal is to gain the call at the first strike price for a credit or only a small debit by selling a pair of calls at the second strike price. Both strike prices will use the same month of expiration.

It is important to keep in mind that there is a very large ceiling for risk in this scenario as if the underlying stock moves more than you have anticipated by a large margin there is nothing protecting your existing interests. As such, you should only try this strategy if you feel only a little bullish as you want the underlying stock to move to the second strike price but them stop completely. If you are not quite as sure what the strength of the market is going to be, the skip strike butterfly call is more appropriate.

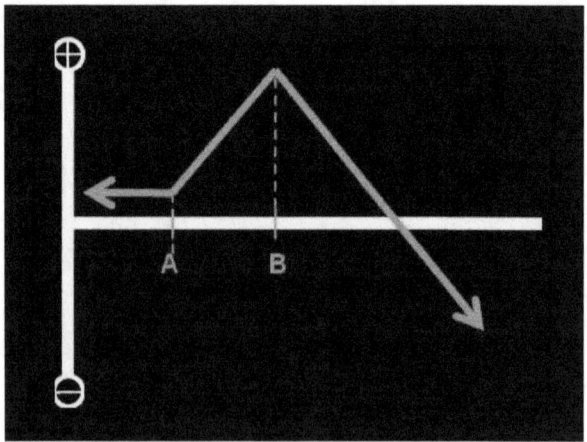

For the best results, you are going to want to see the underlying stock price rise a small amount from the first strike price to the second. This will cover one of the calls that you sold while leaving the second one open to generate more reward, or risk if things do not work out in your favor. As such, it is important to keep a close eye on the underlying stock to ensure that unexpected moves aren't quickly countered and also by having an ironclad stop loss in place, just in case. This risk can further be mitigated by using it with index options as opposed to traditional options because indexes are even less volatile than individual underlying stocks with low volatility because various price movements tend to cancel out major movement in either direction. To use this strategy:

1. You will start by purchasing a call at the first strike price

2. You will then follow that up by selling two calls at a second strike price while understanding the general state of the underlying stock will remain around the first strike point.

Additional considerations
The absolute maximum value that can be gained when using a front spread typically comes the closer it is to expiration. This means that a time frame of no more than 45 days is thought to be the most effective overall. If you prefer not to use uncovered calls, then you can instead buy the underlying stock as a way of establishing this strategy so the second call will not remain uncovered. Remember, when using this strategy, instead of working against you, time decay is working in your favor. While it is still decrease the value of the option that you chose to purchase, that loss will be outweighed by the amount gained from the pair of options that were sold.

Put front spread
The put front spread strategy allows you to buy a put that is either exactly at the money or else slightly out of the money while still paying less than full price for the privilege. If everything goes according to play, then you will get the put in question at the second of two strike prices while generating a credit or at least paying much

less than you otherwise would. This is accomplished by selling a pair of puts at the first of the pair of strike prices.

To get the most out of the transaction you are going to want to see the underlying stock price decrease from the second strike price to the first which means this strategy is at its most effective when you believe the market is in a bearish mood and you expect a small drop in the underlying stock price and a small drop only. This part is important because like the call front spread, only one of the puts that you sold in this strategy is covered which means that if the stock moves drastically compared to what you expected then there is nothing to inherently stop the trade from racking up major losses for you. If you aren't quite sure how much the underlying stock is going to move, the skip strike put butterfly spread is probably the more fiscally advisable option.

Regardless, it is important to keep a close eye on the underlying stock when using this strategy and to never undertake it without having an ironclad stop loss in place, just in case. Like it's call counterpart, the best timeframe for this particular strategy is thought to be anywhere from 30 to 45 days before the expiration of the options in question. To use this strategy:

1. To start using this strategy you want to sell a pair of puts at the first strike price

2. You will then want to purchase a put at the second strike price with the understanding that the underlying stock price is likely to remain above or at this strike price.

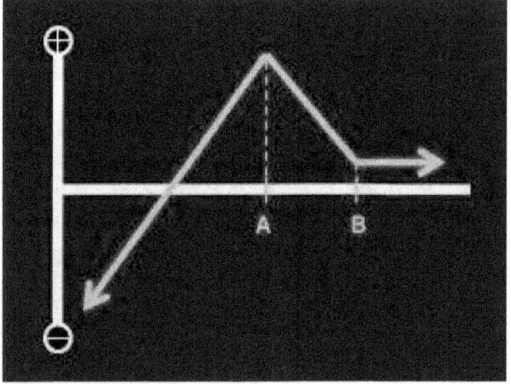

Additional considerations
When using the put front spread you are going to want the underlying stock price to be sitting at the first strike price when the option expires to generate

the most overall profit. The amount of profit that is possible can be determined by finding the difference between the first strike price and the second strike price after any net debts are taken into account. When it comes to the maximum for loss the only limiting factor is to take the first strike price and add the second strike price if the underlying stock continues all the way to zero.

When you are using this strategy your goal is for the implied volatility to decrease as time goes by. This is due to the face that doing so will decrease the value of the options that you sold at likely more than twice the rate that it will affect the option that you purchased as well.

Conclusion

Thank for making it through to the end of *Option Trading: Advanced Tips & Tricks for Your Profit Maximization*, let's hope it was informative and able to provide you with all of the tools you need to achieve your goals both in the near term and for the months and years ahead. Remember, just because you've finished this book doesn't mean there is nothing left to learn on the topic. Truly becoming an expert at something is a marathon, not a sprint, slow and steady wins the race.

The next step is to stop reading already and to put the strategies you've been reading about to good use. While there are always new and improved options trading strategies to learn about, it is important to practice as much as you read, if not more so, practice makes perfect as they say and in this case that means making more profitable trades a greater portion of the time. Only by making the occasional trading mistake can you gain the wisdom that sets the good options traders apart from the greats.

Finally, if you found this book useful in anyway, a review on Amazon is always appreciated!

Here you will find the tools used by me!

- **_Binary Options Trading Signals Live!_**

Binary Options Trading Signals Is The Premier Signal Service For Binary Options As You Watch A Live Trader With Over 10 Years Of Experience! Promote This And Your Users Will Absolutely Love You

- *Binary Options Pro Signals*

Binary Options Pro Signals Is The Best Way To Trade Markets! Customers Love The Product Because Of Its Ease Of Use. Profits Can Be Made In As Little As One Hour.

- *Real Money Doubling Forex Robot Fap Turbo*

Fapturbo Is The Only Automated Forex Income Solution That Doubles Real Monetary Deposits In Under 30 Days.

- *Quantum Binary Signals Subscription*

Quantum Binary Signals Is The Leading Signals Provider For Binary Options Forex, Stocks And Commodities.

Day Trading Series

Day Trading: The Bible - Complete Guide to Crash It With Day Trading
https://www.amazon.com/dp/1534656502

EXTRA BOOK

Fast Memorization Techniques:

Accelerated Learning - Advanced Technique for Fast Learning

JOE BRONSKI

© **Copyright 2016**

All rights Reserved. No part of this book may be reproduced in any form without permission in writing from the author. Reviewers may quote brief passages in reviews.

Disclaimer

No part of this publication may be reproduced or transmitted in any form or by any means, mechanical or electronic, including photocopying or recording, or by any information storage and retrieval system, or transmitted by email without permission in writing from the publisher.

While all attempts have been made to verify the information provided in this publication, neither the author nor the publisher assumes any responsibility for errors, omissions or contrary interpretations of the subject matter herein.

This book is for entertainment purposes only. The views expressed are those of the author alone, and should not be taken as expert instruction or commands. The reader is responsible for his or her own actions.

Adherence to all applicable laws and regulations, including international, federal, state and local laws governing professional licensing, business practices, advertising and all other aspects of doing business in the US, Canada, UK or any other jurisdiction is the sole responsibility of the purchaser or reader.

Neither the author nor the publisher assumes any responsibility or liability whatsoever on the behalf of the purchaser or reader of these materials. Any perceived slight of any individual or organization is purely unintentional.

Introduction

Have you ever wondered what the difference between you and someone who seems to able to endlessly spout facts they have memorized? Or while you were in school why others just seemed to have a much easier time remember facts for tests or were always getting better scores then you? Though some people are just naturally gifted learners the odds are they were taught techniques you were not exposed to and has given them the ability to better retain the information they were taught. They also most likely practiced their techniques keeping their mind sharp and making retention all the easier for their efforts.

There are so many techniques out there for memorization and learning. Some are more effective then others and they all depend on the type of learner you are. This book has been put together to help cover some of the more advanced memorization techniques that can be utilized. Most learning is considered the tradition approach with the student in a more passive role and the teacher will actively put knowledge before the student in an attempt to help them retain the information.

While this has had some success in the past, research has revealed that an accelerated learning approach helps a learner retain more information faster than the tradition techniques. This style encourages the student to become an active participant in their learning as well as helping them truly manipulate the material allowing for total retention in a shorter timeframe. It also allows them to have a much greater grasp of the material because they are forced to place it in their own words and manipulate the information in a way that allows their brain to better understand the concepts they are learning.

This book will go over these techniques in some detail in the hope of helping you become faster and more efficient at memorizing important information. There are different aspects of material that help to determine how difficult it is to study. Theses properties will be discussed as well as strategies that can be used to improve how effectively you can memorize those types of material. We will discuss ways in which you can properly prepare your body for memorization and give you the best chances at retaining the information. It is also believed that seeking a few other sources before you begin your studying can help you give a broader picture and better understanding of what your learning.

Hopefully with the information you are given here, you will be able to efficiently and more completely memorize information that you need to retain. Remember working with your mind is just like working any other muscle in your body. You need to consistently work with it to strengthen the muscle. By applying some of these techniques as well as practicing everyday just like you would if you were an athlete you will be able to better improve your abilities to memorize and retain.

Chapter 1: Why Memorization is Difficult and How to Help Yourself

With research it has been determined that there are about 11 characteristics of information that determine how difficult or easy something is to memorize. Armed with the knowledge of these various characteristics you will hopefully be able to identify why certain knowledge it easier to retain while you struggle in other areas. After you have been given these characteristics will go over strategies that can help you improve memorization with information containing the various characteristics.

- ✓ Abstractness, this characteristic refers to how easy it is to wrap your head around the concept. If the concept is abstract in a nature it will be harder to relate to and make it all the more difficult to put into terms that you will be able to easily understand. The harder an object is to understand the more difficult it is to remember.

- ✓ Complexity, how complex or difficult a problem is can certainly determine how difficult it can be to retain. The more intricate the information the harder it will be for your mind to remember everything in its proper place.

- ✓ Familiarity, is how much exposure you have had to the information you are trying to retain. If you are memorizing information on something you interact with on a day to day basis it will be easier to remember information about it.

- ✓ Humanness, this characteristic refers to how relatable a subject is to the human experiences in life. The more relevance a subject has to being human or experiences we face as human beings the easier it is to relate to and retain.

- ✓ Immediacy, how soon information needs to be retained. The shorter the time frame that information needs to be memorized by the harder or easier it can be to retain depending on your personality.

- ✓ Importance, this characteristic points to how much the information you are trying to memorize impacts your life. The more important it can be to your life in any way can make it easier to remember.

- ✓ Order, the more logical the structure of the information the easier it will be to retain. The more convoluted the information and the harder to decipher its proper order the more difficult it will be for you to remember. Our minds immediately seek to make things easier for us to understand, so if the order doesn't make sense it will be harder for our brains to retain.

- ✓ Relevance, the more useful information will be to you the easier it will be to retain. If its something you can use in your everyday life or can help you in your endeavors the odds are it will be easier to memorize.

- ✓ Salience, when we find information boring it makes it that much harder to focus on the subject. When your bored in class you fall asleep, a similar thing can happen to your brain. When it's bored it can fall asleep in a sense and make it more difficult to retain what your attempting to.

- ✓ Sensuous, how your senses receive the information you want to learn will help to determine how much easier it is to retain. If you can sense it on more planes it is more likely you will be able to remember it.

- ✓ Size, this characteristic can easily be seen as one that helps determine your retention of something. The more their is to retain the more difficult it can be.

Now that we have talked about how these characteristics affect how easy or hard it can be to retain information we will go over ways in which you can improve in areas you might struggle in. If you add characteristics to the material you are trying to retain and you discover a pattern to the types of material you struggle with then you can use these tips to hopefully help you overcome your shortcomings in that retention area.

- ✓ Abstractness, try to relate the information to what's around you. If you can find a way to make it less abstract and easier to relate to the everyday it will be that much easier to remember.

- ✓ Complexity, if you break it down into smaller pieces or simpler steps it can make it easier to understand and retain.

- ✓ Familiarity, try to review information more frequently. If you can try to review it for a short amount of time every day. The more you are exposed to it the more familiar you will be with it.

- ✓ Humanness, turn your information in a story and try to make yourself the main character. Not only will it help you relate the information to something more natural. By making yourself the star it will be all the more interesting to remember.

- ✓ Immediacy, setting yourself a deadline to have information retained by can help keep you motivated even if you don't need it for any particular time. Sometimes if you don't need it for a test or something similar you may procrastinate on the material in question.

- ✓ Importance, try to set a goal or objective to memorizing the information. If you can make it more important to yourself, it will be easier to retain.

- ✓ Order, if you struggle to remember information and the order makes no sense simply restructure it in a way that makes sense to you. You will then be able to better retain the information.

- ✓ Relevance, if you figure out a way in which it can be relevant to your life it will make it easier to retain.

- ✓ Salience, try to create a story to go along with the information. If you can string the information together in a funny or crazy way it will not only be more memorable but it will keep it more interesting.

- ✓ Sensuous, if you can only associate your information with one sense you may find it harder to retain but if you try to find other sense that it can relate to you will find it easier to remember. It may take a little creativity to figure out how to engage other senses but it can be a big help.

- ✓ Size, if you have a large amount of material to cover break it down into smaller chunks to give your brain a more manageable chunk of information to remember.

When memorizing information most people use familiarity in order to retain information. Others who are better at retaining information.

Chapter 2: Preparing Your Body

One of the most important things you can do to help you become a memorization wiz is to take care of yourself. By ensuring that your system is running at its best you will give your mind the best shot possible to retain information. A body that is sleep deprived or not given the proper fuel will not function as well as one that is. So by following a few of these simple steps you will set your mind up for success and making learning and retaining what you have learned that much easier.

Get enough sleep, it cannot be stressed enough how important sleep is. Try to get at least 7 hours of sleep a day, a well rested mind is more prepared to retain information and is just more ready to work in general. Also minimize your blue light exposure before going to sleep, so avoid computers, your phones, and TV before bed.

Try to keep yourself well hydrated. If you can keep water or maybe even some unsweetened tea, sugar will defeat the exercise, your body and brain will be able to better function getting the water that it needs to live off of.

Sugar can be your enemy in the case of studying, it may seem like a great jolt to keep you going but the crash can stop you in your tracks and make things worse for you. The excess energy can be the wrong kind making your more fidgety then able to sit and focus like you may need to.

Walk or exercise on a regular basis if you can. The better your body function the healthier you will feel and your brain will feel. You are also more likely to feel happier and better about yourself and this lift in mood can make focusing and studying that much easier.

Try to avoid stressors and schedule out your day to a certain degree so you can reach optimal productivity during your day. Not only will you feel like you have accomplished something it will help keep you from stressing about things you need to accomplish because you will already be preparing your brain.

Chapter 3: A Few Other Techniques

In this day and age there are far too many distractions available to take our attention away from the tasks at hand. But if you would like to be able to memorize information faster and become a better learner there are a few techniques you can employ to help you double or even triple the amount of information you can retain in your sessions. When you allow yourself to be distracted you make it that much harder for your brain to simple take in the information you are presenting it. With those other distractions joking for the position of attention in your mind it will force you to work that much harder to try and remember.

If you are a music lover try to listen to music without lyrics. Music with lyrics can interfere with your language processing abilities. So when you listen to music with lots of lyrics you're essentially sabotaging yourself. Your brain will be unable to totally focus on one set of information because the other will either be spoken or read and disrupt the flow of the other. So instead try to listen to music that is only instrumental. If you can stay away from music that has any lyrics your can still listen to sounds in the background without distracting yourself from the material and make learning and retention that much easier.

Try to choose times that are most conducive to studying. If you choose to work when you are very likely to be interrupted, you will easily be distracted with each interruption and make it that much harder for yourself. Also shoot for times with your have energy. If you are tired your mind is likely to be clear and able to engage in the types of mental gymnastics you are asking of it. You would never ask you body to run a marathon when you are exhausted so why ask the same of your brain? It is a muscle too. By keeping distractions to a minimum and being properly energized you are also less likely to experience stress while studying which can also make it easier on yourself. The more stressed you are the harder it will be to concentrate on the task at hand.

With the technology available to us it can be extremely hard to disconnect from everything and everyone around us. By having a cellphone, you are totally accessible to everyone at all times. This constant connection can be so distracting, talking with your friends or finding out what someone just posted on Facebook can be so much more engaging then the studying you are trying to accomplish. But if you want to be able to memorize and retain the information you are working with you need to do yourself a favor and unplug from everything around you. Turn off notifications, your cell phone, whatever you need to do to be totally focused on the task at hand. This can be very hard for some people especially if they have never done it before. If this is the case for you try for about 20 minutes at a time. You don't want to drive yourself to distraction by being unplugged because that wont achieve anything either.

Many people studying sitting or laying down. While this restful state can help keep you focused on one thing and one thing only you also don't want to completely sit like a lump the whole time. Standing and walking around for short breaks can help promote blood flow and even energy into your body. Both are helpful for keeping you fresh and focused. You also provide more oxygen to your brain from the increased blood flow and the more oxygen your brain has the better it will function.

Prioritize the material you are about to review. If say you feel very confident on certain parts of the information you are cover then you should skip those parts and review what you are shakier with. When you go over material you are already very familiar with you can give yourself a false sense of security. You will feel like you know more and take time away from the information that really needs your attention. It will also increase your exposure to what you are unfamiliar with helping you to each maximum retention of all the topics you are trying to remember.

Tell yourself a story. This is one that can't be stressed enough, if you can find a story to help show you the information you are trying to learn that's excellent and you should read it. But if you can make one up, by placing information into a relatable story your brain will have an easier time remember that then trying to chock down random bits of information. Telling your story to someone else or even attempting to teach them material will also help you to better retain it. When you teach someone else you are forced to reword the information and put it into each to understand bites for someone who doesn't know the material. This rewording and forcing you to really work with the concepts will give you a better understanding and make it that much easier to understand.

The last tip to keep in mind is to try and preview the content you are about to go over. By going on other websites or searching in other books before getting down to some serious studying or memorization you can help to give yourself perspective on material that might not necessarily be clear from the source you are currently reading. It can make things clearer it can also give you different perspective that can help the information to click in your mind and help you to remember it better. You can also give yourself a bigger picture if you skim before you read in detail. You will better be able to see where the text is heading and hopefully by causing that light of recognition in your brain you will be reinforcing some pathways in your brain.

Conclusion

Thank you for downloading this book. There is a lot of information out there just waiting to be retained for you to use later or apply to your everyday life. So why would you want to wait or let everything that there is to learn out their pass you by? The world is full of so much knowledge and now with some of the techniques in this book anyone can start memorizing information like a pro.

Try to work through all the techniques in this book and don't forget about a few life style changes you can make to help improve your health and your mind. You can neglect one part of yourself and still expect to get the same results so remember to give all parts a try to get the best results possible.

It is our hope that you were able to get all the information you could need from this book and we hope that you will share your experiences with others. By reviewing this book not only will you be helping others with their decisions you will also being giving us invaluable feedback to help us keep improving any more information we try to provide in the future. Your feedback is so important to us and we value your opinion as our avid customer.